LIGHTNING TREE

LIGHTNING
TREE

POEMS BY
JOHN
KINSELLA

2003

Published by Arc Publications
Nanholme Mill, Shaw Wood Road
Todmorden, Lancs OL14 6DA, UK

Design by Tony Ward
Printed at the Arc & Throstle Press Ltd
Nanholme Mill, Shaw Wood Road
Todmorden, Lancs OL14 6DA, UK

ISBN 1 900072 61 0

Lightning Tree was first published
in 1996 by Fremantle Arts Centre Press.

Some of the poems in this volume
were previously published in:
*Antipodes, Australian, FAR, Heat, Imago,
International Quarterly, Iowa Review,
Island, Landfall, LinQ, Paris Review,
Poetical Histories, Prairie Dog, Salt,
Sightings, Southerly, Takahe,
The Canberra Times, The Western Review*
and *Windsor Review.*

The author acknowledges the Literature
Board of the Australia Council for a
Senior Fellowship during which many of
these poems were written.

Cover photographs: Kate Mellor

The publishers acknowledge financial
assistance from Arts Council of England, Yorkshire

Arc Publications International Poets
Series Editor: John Kinsella

To my mother,
Wendy J. Kinsella

CONTENTS

A SHORT TOUR OF THE COCOS ATOLL

THE COCONUT STORY

when the old man found the coconut
the coconut with no eyes found in the cemetery
he kept it & soon found a cousin's stolen stuff
& said the coconut will sort it out

the coconut with no eyes found in the cemetery
told Mancep – the magic man – the thief will return it
& said the coconut will sort it out
but tell no one or the magic will be undone

told Mancep – the magic man – the thief will return it
the coconut without eyes sees everything & speaks truth
but tell no one or the magic will be undone
the coconut expects those helped to give something back

the coconut without eyes sees everything & speaks truth
so the owner of the islands hears this & wants the coconut
the coconut expects those helped to give something back
but the owner wants to take the power away for himself

so the owner of the islands hears this & wants the coconut
Mancep says this is not the will of the coconut
but the owner wants to take the power away for himself
Mancep says a great disaster will come his way

Mancep says this is not the will of the coconut
though the owner takes it over the seas with him
Mancep says a great disaster will come his way
though for six years they hear nothing

though the owner takes it over the seas with him
he cannot control the power for the power is great
though for six years they hear nothing
& the people think the power has gone with him

he cannot control the power for the power is great
& he dies & his family brings the body back
& the people think the power has gone with him
because there is trouble & discontent everywhere

& he dies & his family brings the body back
though a great storm wrecks the ship
because there is trouble & discontent everywhere
because in the coffin was the coconut which the sea frees

though a great storm wrecks the ship
Mancep sees the coconut washed up on the beach
because in the coffin was the coconut which the sea frees
for Mancep to take back & set things right.

A SHORT TOUR OF THE COCOS ATOLL

From Rumah Baru the runabout
skips over the rippling tidal sweep,
the lift & drop of the hull's skin
like the crack of a sail full blown,
dead, full blown again. We traverse
sinkholes cool with depth,
almost black like inverted islands
set in intertidal reef,
a sub-surface map
where intensity of colour
makes do for sonar.
Ashore on Pulu Labu –
the sheet anchor claws the sand,
a few chickens idle nearby.
On the island's ocean side
I lacerate my feet on splintered coral,
collect a composite rubber sheet
from which a dozen pairs of children's
thongs have been pressed somewhere
in Indonesia, brought by the tides
& currents to Cocos. A brown booby
glides high overhead,
the humid atmosphere
muffling its call – these birds
nest on North Keeling
which is out of reach, but are treasured
by the Cocos Malays as a delicacy,
a food for which the Federal police
will often travel to Home Island
to investigate a rumoured feast.
Jeff is busy casting a net
for bait fish, he hauls
in a small school & collects
the anchor. I squirm with the fish:
they flick at my feet as I grip

the gunwale. Jeff
steers towards Pulu Kambang
& I can tell he's
checking me out – test
the weird vegetarian
who lets fish go & loves
the orange & black concertinaed
bodies of sea-slugs, who
jumps onto the reef & tows
the runabout with unnaturally long legs.
The tide's retreat is in full swing.
We anchor a couple of ks from the beach.
Mud crabs bubble just below the flat.
Stands of driftwood lurk like booby traps.
Jeff chases reef sharks in knee-deep hollows
& tries to beach them. Their black tips race
towards dry land & dart suddenly
back to the depths. They are quicker than Jeff.
We walk to the island & walk back again.
The sun devastates our skin.
We suffer mutually.
Jeff heads for deep water
& says he wants to spear the treasured green fish.
He dives like a wounded frigate
& returns with nothing.
He is popular on Home Island
& speaks with thirty years
behind him. He is not the West Islander now.
And this is how I like him.
Returning to Rumah Baru
I wonder if he's the man the Cocos Malays
have been seeing – or almost seeing – shadowing
the coconut groves. Appearing at special moments,
bringing good luck.

It's little wonder the Home Islanders
want to keep this mob off their island.
Drinkers living in each other's pockets
with a language all their own.
Even those on short tours –
which often become shorter tours –
pick up a kind of addled strine.
They work on 'Cocos Time',
wear as little as possible,
& look forward to the charter
jet's arrival. They form societies
that parody the mainland & drink duty-free
liquor at the Club. *Rumour* is their neighbour
so most aspire to owning a boat –
getting out into the ocean
where they can't be seen – the irony
of a small community in isolation.
West Island with its land & ghost crabs,
bantam chooks darting in & out
of the coconut palms. Its Sydney highway
as thin as a fanbelt & a whole 7ks long,
the high-pitched drone of ex-postal bikes
& nights out in the Cocos Lodge Mess.
Mick, husband of Ali (sometimes
secretary to visiting writers),
is a great cook who dreams
of setting up in a posh restaurant
on the mainland. Ali misses Kenya
but loves the life on Cocos.
They also have a boat & like a drink.
Hosai cooks a good chilli dish.
His chillies are grown hydroponically
at West Island's very own

market garden. Lettuces the size of fists
grow there. But then in-micro
so do many other things.
But most people pay extra
to have fresh veges flown
up from Perth – broccoli
& cauliflower that look like coral.
Oh, the Club is also the cyclone shelter
so if things look really bad
like during the 1909 cyclone
which destroyed 90 per cent
of the coconut palms
& demolished most of the houses
on Home Island, then no doubt
all will hit the bar & die pissed.
The military make fleeting visits
but people don't speak
too much of these unless
they've had a few too many.
Don't forget, the girl next to you
at the pub might be one
of the hospital's nurses
& know more about you
than you think.
At the Quarantine Station
they keep sterile chooks
to warn of undetected
diseases. Lately ostriches
have been the go – Australians
& Canadians at each other's throats
over who owns the chicks. The Feds
are even taking an interest.
The Cocos Indus Malay

Restaurant has started
a fish & chip night.
A couple of kids have painted
the school walls. The feral dive shop
has closed early – Dieter, 'good bloke he is',
watches that tourists don't dive too deep.
And JCR, no longer the boss,
sells ornamental shells to the Japanese.
He's not such a bad bloke but won't tell
any secrets. The Cocos Malays
say he knows the spirits.
The West Islanders reckon
he holds the best parties
& tells great jokes.

INDIAN OCEAN ODE

The long arms of a cyclonic nebula
whip coconut palms into a trance-like frenzy.
The remaining ironwood – stunted – cut back
for carvings, firewood, & boats –
snarls. Cabbage bush and pandanus
heave & shudder. Coral cays
suffer damage on the fringes,
the relentless assault of the seas
grinding the living tips
of the volcanic sea mount.
Heavy rain covers freshwater lenses
in their coral sand aquifers
like sets of contacts.
Even iron drums
filled with gelatinous
palm oil seethe, bubbles speaking
with a voice as syrupy as cholesterol.
Fish dive deep into sinkholes,
the lagoon froths & whinges
against the coral. Boats
break their moorings.

A bright morning makes a liar
of the water's dark orchestrations.
The loyalties of small communities
(linked only by slow-boats & slow-to-come
air-charters, where a population
gathers at the airstrip to see what's new
or drink themselves to death among
the tourists at the social club),
are sorely tested, all lines

of communication
being down.
The sky is clear
& below the ocean's surface
Moorish idols perform coralline
rituals. Parrotfish graze quietly.
The coral, in its atmosphere
of fish & anemones, univalved
& bivalved predators, rip & dart
of reef sharks, repairs itself
& builds outwards.
On the surface
signs of the cyclone
are everywhere – a tangled carpet
of palm leaves, household debris, & even
the leeward islands littered
with flotsam & jetsam.
Land crabs re-emerge
from the undergrowth
to devour new layers of leaf litter,
Council workers & house owners
kick through the wreckage,
recaptured boats sail reefwards
where gorgonian fan corals
wave delicately
& the Indian Ocean settles
like amniotic fluid around
the *myth of origin*.

Heartbreak Drive, Cocos's Boulevard
of Broken Dreams, where all New York 'gals'
would *love to* be, attracts love-struck tourists
as if it were pure paradise. From Cocos
Hospital (where they recover from reef cuts
& alcohol), to Unjung Tanjong (where the ferry
takes them over the coral-encrusted lagoon
for brief outings on Home Island where an eyeless
coconut sees their every move & each grain
of sand has a name & is part of a family, where
a story is born with every sunset & Allah
stretches over the Indian Ocean towards Mecca),
all muse over the irony of a name. Like 'Lover's
Leap', which in any place, they'll maintain,
must be a place of magnetic beauty. I tell them
this coconut-palmed road that leads to snow-white
tropical sands is the place where infidelities
are named, where twelve-month contracts
are reduced to six & whole families book
their flights home. Where a long-term
Westerner might say to another 'There's
no room for suicides here' or 'No room
for *singles* on these islands.' There should be signs
along the boulevard – neon flirting with moonless
nights, like New York or somewhere else
that's thick with people & seen as a place
as far away from paradise as you can get.

COCOS DOLDRUMS

Incestuous, the tunes of air stilled
by doldrums. Becalmed on tiny islands,
you can hear the coral breathing all around,
especially on the higher ground,
still just a metre or so above sea level.

The configurations of land crabs
are logographic – you get to read
the weather signs by the number
crushed on the roads: wet weather
& ennui send them crazy, the psychotic
rustle like static in the undergrowth
sending residents troppo –
stir-crazy & ready to snap.

Tourists flounder in the mess
& watch Australia Television,
sipping black tea. The fans whir
at take-off speed. Cigarette smoke
makes non-smokers filthy.
They eye their fellow guests
dangerously.

The bar is over-the-top
in the evenings. Relationships
are broken, few are made,
& though 'no one fights here'
I find myself bending my jaw & glasses
back into shape.

DOGS

Only JCR has a dog on Cocos.
They tell me on West Island
dogs are an eco problem.
His dog is old & everybody
likes it. But there are many cats –
there to keep the rats down.
Which *breed like mad*.
On Home Island I'm told that dogs
are unclean. Tourists, given the chance,
would enter Cocos Malay houses
without taking their shoes off,
interrupt prayer times.

SCANDAL

outside the administrator's compound they sit
on worn metal peacock chairs watching a sunset
which changes from blood red to a high-altitude tropical snow:
from the motorbike parked outside her window the boss
guesses what's going on & then after a few drinks knows
but this is what she wants, the rumours to travel quickly
to the Q Station just to let him know she's had enough
& he'd better listen – but like the sunset there are contradictions
in its determined show, & the tropics will have their cold snaps
even if you don't feel them.

23

ESSAY ON RUMOURS

The night movements of land crabs
rumour a new resident as the atoll
wheels into place under the plane's
touchdown. Watches move
indiscernibly when set
to Cocos time, where conjecture
exists like the delay on the telephone
as the satellite works against the logic
of there being land in the middle
of the Indian Ocean, building
like a theory of coral reef formation
over the plummeting depths
as a coconut falls
& kills someone whose name
becomes a section of slowly expanding
palm grove. The bark of geckoes
beautifully lilting
when out of earshot
enhances the richness of gossip:
the tour gathering slowly its tropical
momentum like prejudice,
like going back to an earlier draft
& finding it barely resembles
the final product. *It's been heard
that he's going out with ... on Christmas ...*
as a teacher in the Jungle Bar
suggests they talk about Dransfield
on Cocos Indian Ocean radio,
but moves closer to his girlfriend
when asked if he's read the poems.
Delivered by the structured currents
Javanese thong pressings flap
on the perimeters of tiny islands:
compound sheets of rubber
with die-pressed spaces.

Outside the Administrator's
pseudo-mansion that says *we're not
Clunies Ross but still in charge here*
rumour sits on *that* worn metal
peacock chair & obsesses
the sunset, the sky so clear
it swallows even the deep red
of the tropical orb. Allen,
a 'six-monther', reckons
that despite the constant turnover,
things hang together. Rumour
has it he's not welcome
where he came from,
but on Cocos he's dead popular,
keeping a level head,
not one for gossip.

Eight years old & making sugar
from coconuts & climbing the springy
trunks of coconut trees to drop the fruit

then fishing the white fish – sweet lip
Kap Kaying – if Allah says you are lucky
then you catch a fish after just one minute

basket weaving in my spare time
taught by my father who like me
spent all of his life on Home Island

he was a first-class carpenter
& the fruits of his labour
are everywhere

I did not marry which is good
because there are many who want to marry
but because the island is so small

& there are few of us marriage
is not always possible – I live
in my brother's house, & he has children

I swim when the current is strong
& the tide is running out of the lagoon,
I test my strength by going against it

I like football but do not watch television & now I make jewellery: earrings
and brooches out of coconut shell

& spider shell & cowrie too – these islands
are only coral & shell & coconut
but once they were jungle & thick with birds

& because the Japanese might come
in their boats that should not have
sailed we built huts for soldiers

from Ceylon on Horsburgh Island
& I was cook & I sailed on a jakung
there and back every day from Home Island

because the boss made me & when
the wind went into hiding I rowed
across & on a Saturday in 1945

the Japanese bombed Pica Delly
& the house I was in exploded & I ran scared
carrying nephews under each arm

while twenty-seven houses burnt
& a woman & a boy lay dying
& because of the bombing

only I finished the Koran
in Arabic, the others could not finish
& we also hid on Pulu Ampang

because there were no houses
for the Japanese to bomb
& after the war I spent my time

demolishing military houses
that were left over & then made boats
with John Cecil Clunies Ross

the King of Cocos who we liked
'cause he didn't say he owned us
& was very polite & made

the coconut work for everyone
but then his wife said there
were too many people on the island

& some went to Borneo & Singapore
& many others to Christmas Island
which is in the middle of the same

great ocean as the Cocos Keeling Islands
& owned by JCCR as well & young boys
were sent to work the phosphate mine

but their families were unhappy
so JCCR sent them as well but the Chinese
took the contract & some came back

& later others were taken by the Government
down to Perth. Now I tell you my life
because you will tell others –

Cocos is a small place but there
are many stories & none
are forgotten.

AN ESCAPE FROM THE GARDENS
OF OCEANIA HOUSE

That in this garden where a talking tree
once translated destiny, where hibiscus
& rose garnished all manner of fruits,
Bertha, a mistress of John Sydney,
spat at Biong as he looked up at her
perched in the jambu tree.
Cursing the ivory tokens
he worked daily long & hard for,
being told what he could & couldn't do,
he stole a boat with Emon
& set sail for the thickets of West Island.
And though hunted down,
shot & speared, he would not die
until Nek Icang removed the 'magic sash'
from around his waist.

FIRE ANTS

They're loading
ostriches on a DC9 tonight
in a fierce wind
that carries the high-pitched
whine of turbos
into your room.
A gecko barks
& makes the place
feel more alien
than it is. The sea
grinds against iron
& stone pushed onto the beach
after the Second World War.
You can almost sense coconut shoots
retreating back into their seeds.
Ghost crabs twist crazily on the sands.
Fire ants burn trails
across the floor towards
an uneaten dinner
like strands of petrified & aged
lightning – lustreless
but still dangerous.
One of the locals
has failed to return
from a fishing trip. You think
of that story a friend
from Home Island was telling you –
that there lives on the inland
side of Gunung – the mountain sand dune
of South Island – an evil setan
who collects the spirits
of those lost in Cocos seas –
& you think of the dukuns
who know the spirit world,
whether or not they could tell you

if this spirit has hold of the fisherman's soul,
if a search party is needed –
but the last ferry between the islands
has long since left so you concentrate
beyond the drone of the aircraft
& study the fire ants in their
unwavering task – lifelines
across the room.

LETTER TO ROSALI

Hey Home Boy, what's happening
in your neck of the woods?
Or, should I say, in your patch
of coconut palms, on your slice
of beach, your chunk of coral?
Still working on those aerials –
keeping the info-flow steady
through Cocos? I reckon
those things attract rumours
like sharks around the fishing
boats, bet gossip has been
running hot as usual.
Well, I missed Hari Raya Puasa
so you'll have to write
& let me know how much weight
everyone put on – after a month
of fasting it seemed a different people
had populated the islands.
I tell you, I really miss
the friendliness of the place –
maybe it's a friendliness
that comes with living
so close together & having to get on –
what do you think?
I was in India recently
& went searching for coconuts.
They weren't quite the same
but were still good. Somebody's
reading over my shoulder
& telling me 'good'
is not really a 'word',
but I know you who
showed me the heart
of the coconut palm
understand what I mean,

you who made me good
after my blood
stained your sari,
you who showed me how to wrap
myself against those who
would use me, who
could make a 'millionaire's salad',
who on Tupung Jalan said
to that part of the island 'excuse me,
I'm on your territory,
can I pass?' who said
that Cocos Malays say
exactly what they mean –
& that it would be good
when Cocos became
its own boss.

Rosali, may your
penunggu watch closely
over you & your family,
& may all penunggu of island & sea
combine their powers
& make good magic
for you all. No shadow puppet
moves without help.

LITTLE PICARESQUE

HEADING SOUTH THROUGH
THE LONG PADDOCK

for Tom Flood and Dorothy Hewett

On the last day of November
I journey to see my brother,
the tyres sticky on the asphalt
as the ground thunders
with grain trucks.
The fly-blown carcasses
of kangaroos fester like boils
and I think of the times
I worked on the wheatbins,
two seasons in hell,
trapped in a hut with a bunch
of boys who had to be *boys*
even though they probably
found it hell as well.
It leads me to think of Tom Flood,
and his mother Dorothy
who grew up in this territory,
who set the dead sea of wheat
against itself, growing green
under the sapping sun
long before belly-dumpers
and tip-trucks rolled
along this road. The grain here
is mainly oats and barley
though some wheat spills
from the augers – but not Oceana Fine,
which belongs to another place
and another time. Soon I'll hear
how the cover of my book
was ripped from its spine
by some Nyoongah mates
of my brother's – they reckon

that tractors and ploughs
are bad for the land,
and they are right.
But this is the heritage
I bring with me,
and there's no denying it.
The windrows layer the hills
like enormous elegant snakes –
the art of humans is always
deceptive. I shouldn't be 'saying' this
but intimating or illustrating
by allusion or association –
I should find a new language
that will burrow deep
into the conscience,
as if it were a maggot
in a sheep or kangaroo carcass,
as if the conscience
were a piece of mangled meat
hit again and again by trucks.
Knocking some sense into it
some smart arse might say.
But this language would have to be
like everything I see,
but understood by those
who can't or haven't seen.
For it's them I'd want to tell.
For it's a story, it's my story
as well. Like eucalypt blossom
luminous in the upper atmosphere,
like another season laying
itself over this one,
like unspoken family histories
that might account for it
but don't need to. I pass

a silo, and a dead numbat.
They're rare, and the stripes
are like a warning. Later
my brother will tell me
there've been heaps
around this season; he's
been out in the bush
with his girlfriend, maybe
near the Devil's Backbone,
which is a place sacred
to her people, but now called
what the farmers in the district
call it. And as I drive
through the long paddock
glass wheat stalks deflect the sun
and the paddocks shimmer;
dams glower like blue windows
in a false surface. The long paddock –
where sheep are grazed in a hard season,
where dogs working the space
between fence and road –
a red-capped parrot sits
among a flock of twenty-eights.
And nearby, wandoo brilliantly white
strikes the already hollowing sky,
while dense stands of mallet –
once an industry in Narrogin –
stand bolt upright, seeded
onto chained scrubland,
the moon like a damaged ball-joint,
crops fox-red, hawks over the hay.
Here, with only the wind
rushing through the car window,
my language is of sight

and words merely compressions
of what I see: parrot flocks
seething on the ragged edge
of a soon-to-be-harvested crop,
the header comb set low
and a crew getting ready
to spot that night. The images
crash into each other. Distantly
an old Nyoongah woman sings echidnas
out of their tree-stump hollows,
balled and spined
they walk out, struck by the song.
The wheels hit a rupture in the road.
I struggle to maintain control.
Everything here is like something else
because it is not as it was.

SHE-OAKS

We had assumed
them dead – brittle and raw umber
against the olive and ochre
waves of pasture stripped
and sucked dry
by locusts.

Now, two seasons later,
it is almost winter
and mustard needles
are blanketing
the surrounding ground –
full quotas that mock
our glibness, bring
to mind the first
viridian tips
that stopped the tractor
with chain and hooks
dead in its tracks.

RAT TUNNELS IN THE WALL
OF THE HORSE DAM

Like monks tunnelling into desert
mesas, a vibrant hermitage surrounded
by a moat of sand, rats have tunnelled
deep into the walls of the horse dam.

But their science is flawed – it's Autumn
now and the rains have yet to come,
Summer lies low in the hollowed ground,
a brackish indolent puddle – Winter

will unleash the flood that will fill
the lowest chambers, drive rats with young
blindly towards the upper galleries,
as frenzied as victims in disaster films

who've realised technology is just a mask
to hide a human failing – 'we can't be wrong.
we've considered every alternative.' But God
makes kingdoms in the strangest places.

SPRING FEVER

Sawdust soaked in kerosene,
storm-fallen wood, ash-flurries
over the stoked bed of a dead fire.

Dawn air bites like a solvent
as crazy kids race ringneck parrots
whipping motorbikes

into frenzies.
Fog steams over
the house dam

& long-legged waterbirds
preen ahead of the sun's
arrival. The talk

is of rat hunts
in the old sheds
late the night before,

lengths of poly-pipe –
the weapons –
buried guiltily

under sheafs of straw.
Today they will shoot
at their old man's *empties*.

'Hear Jeff hooning in late last night?
Mum says he's got Spring fever –
been at the pub every night

this week.' The sun
drags the fog, chips
of sedimentary rock

skip across the water –
the rings of their contact
echoing softly.

THINKING BACK TO LAST YEAR'S FLOODS

The impact of dipping deep into the floodway,
level ground suddenly plateau'd & top-plated
with redgum, upturned quivers of she-oak
arrowing, while down down sheep tracks run
against the tannic tea-tree rub, down through riven
sandstone, onto the spreading flood plain. It being
summer now, you drown in flies & dust, heat
merging with the flashpast of cars
& grain trucks. Above, the foliage canopy
contracts in shade, crimson rosellas step back
in unison, a tidal rush that suggests shadows
within shadows, the current beneath the haze's
surface, beneath the rip of willy-willies tossing
up a storm, separating the traffic's haze
like floodwaters or a violent memory.

HALFLIGHT

I walk the waterlogged paddocks,
vapours welling up out of the graves,
twitching and pulsing in the halflight.

The fenceline trembles as a flock
of city slickers feels its way back
to the homestead – armed to the teeth

with skulls and bones of sheep.
I move away, drawing my collar
close to my neck. When they've passed

I'll check on the gates – one left open
can result in the death of stock
or destruction of an entire crop.

I wonder at their booty – the picked-over
skeletons of lambs lost to frost or foxes,
old ewes shot in the paddocks as the cancer

ate into their bowels. I wonder
as evening closes on my steps, the remains
of my family just below the surface,

what becomes of those who remove
bones from their places of rest.

LOCUSTS

for David Ray

That soon they'll move
down into the city
descending
the tree-thick scarp,
the last line
of defence. Motorists
talk of locusts falling in showers,
fuming in waves,
spattering car grilles & windscreens,
the ooze from their bodies
eating away at the paint.
Crops have been stripped
to the ground,
trees shaved back to the bone,
& ibises so full
they are ploughed down
on the roads.
Reports of shade cloth
& towels & canvas awnings
being consumed in the frenzy,
of folk using their last water
to ward off the swarms
fill the news bulletins –
mice last year,
this year locusts –
subeditors scanning Bibles
frantically for titles
despite scientists
indicting
the weather.

FILM SHOOT

A friend rang to see if was okay for a mate to take his film crew up to Wheatlands for an on-location shoot. I'm told he's hell-bent on finding a typical farm for the scene where the young bloke leaves the family property 'cause his dad's had a stroke and times are tough and they need extra money just to keep food in the family's mouth. He reckons they need shots of machinery lumbering across hostile turf, tree stumps being ripped out of the ground and burned in unholy bonfires, dogs gnashing at the hind legs of sheep. I tell him that a film crew went up to Wheatlands a quarter of a century ago to capture the first growth of trees planted in a bid to reclaim ground lost to salt. That only storm-fallen wood is burned. That there have been no dogs on the property for years. That the guns are silent.

FALNASH

hot winds cut the verandahs,
tin peels in waves
shaving the jarrah timbers

dishevelled pines
undress
from their tops down

stark cores puncturing
even
the lightest of clouds

there is no little England here:
the dead generations
have not returned to claim

this decaying mansion on the hill:
& as my brother's didgeridoo
booms & warbles, shrills & hums

all time runs like echoes
back & forth across fields & gullies,
eucalypt stands & granite outcrops

at night the wind holds
sheets of newspaper
over paneless windows

& fire bricks grin
like bloody
gargoyles

my brother has invited
the spirits of tea-tree gullies
into his house

once, during an absence
debil-debils came
& held a seance

red hessian & brilliant camellias
augment winter's constantly
burning hearth – the cold here

is bitter, even fruit trees
grow an extra cutaneous layer,
chilblains & lichen

their layers of clothing,
quinces & nectarines
strikes of ball lightning

suspended in frost,
crows dancing & stropping
metallic-grey beaks

on the windlass
of the finely stoned well,
its waters clean & sharp

between seasons
the garden is dug
& planted

the soil friable
& full
& nutritious

an empire of rodents:
food is suspended in sacks
from roof beams

their share is left
in chipped & scarred china
by the door

sometimes the rednecks come
with their guns & cross-haired telescopics
utes & spotlights & cartons of beer

'Shoot Ferals' their engines
rev & throb, slugs ricocheting
from Falnash's solid walls

& as they race down
the gravel track, their hoots
trailing like exhaust

the wind carries
the deeply drawn crow-calls
up through the heavy fruit.

SEPARATIONS

1

Fitting
      that it should happen
here.
      The red carpet no more
than a sheet of Roundup.
But death is like that,
and a grave is not
the solid entry we'd
like to think –
      light-filled
proscenium nurturing
its
   vapid traffic.

2

You can't bring yourself
      to think
something should happen.
There's no tension
in the moment. Movement
does not impel. True,
the rich bronze field
may tomorrow
      succumb
to fire, but who's
      to say?

3

Fluid, the husks of wild oats
chime like rain on a thin
but solid surface –
                    their barbed
offspring
          choking your socks.
There is a voice as well.
You recognise it but can't
bring yourself to look up,
                            reply.

4

And don't look back either –
                            there's no link
between fate and highly-strung
flocks of cockatoos stripping
peach and nectarine, or the duality
of reflections dancing back along
the guttering, leaving water in tanks
rippling shadow and air. Light
                            galvanises
against
          the necessary
fall.

5

A chip of quartz
                    skips
across
        the
                muddy
                        waters
of the dam. You lift
an observation from
                        another
paddock: a semitrailer
overladen with hay bales
rocks on its axels, a two-faced wind
singing *luff luff*
                    against
the crazy strands,
the remains of the crop
surging
        against the wheels.
The chip of quartz reaches
the far bank. Satisfied,
you separate
                the scenes.

LIKE AWKWARD BLUE SMOKE

Like awkward blue smoke
with enveloping wings
the white-faced heron
attempts lift & falters
from the garden dam
near the house
on the back road
where the child stepped out
from the verandah
into the path
of a laden semitrailer
twenty harvests ago,
the salmon gums
running deep pink
in the late
afternoon.

EAGLE

Even from the back of a pick-up
cruising rough gravel roads its launch
can be heard, that 'unnatural quiet'

before the crack of its wings,
like the farmer, slowly squeezing
the rifle's trigger, his body dead

calm – trying to knock one off
on the quiet, 'been at my lambs' he
reckons. There is something

about the wind-up of an eagle about to lope
into flight over bone-white paddocks in midsummer,
its wings the colour of heat-tortured copper,

the beak the curve of the well-honed kill-
knife, testing its keenness with a crosshair,
its talons trailing like viscera.

ANATHALAMION

My parents dead & the family property
broken up, I live on *their* place – in the old shearing
quarters – & keep an eye on things. Talking
business with the old man is impossible though the old lady
comes to the quarters once a week & we sit with a cuppa & study
the week's takings – sorting out the bills & tallying
the red & black figures. She's always been good
with numbers. But it's like she's given up caring
about things really – just working the sums to trade
away the bad memories. The old man sits in a hide
down by the creek some days – watching the blue heron
high in the redgum tree that was blasted
by lightning years back. When I go to the hotel
they ask me what the old couple do these days but I just get plastered
& stare into my beer – snubbing even the mayor – 'to Hell!
with the lot of you!' I'll yell, just waiting for a quarrel.
On a dark day, when the season was closing in,
they were seen leaving the town, like the blue heron.

After their son's death the blue heron became the old man's obses-
sion and his wife told me he only ever spoke to her when talking of
them. The blue heron, their nest raided by crows, have left the
redgum this year. I like to think they're nesting nearby – maybe
further upcreek where the redgums are still thick. Their son had
once claimed that he'd been told by a hay stooker that if you died
near a heron your soul joined with its soul. He'd told that to his
parents and they'd laughed. He marvelled that it was called a blue
heron when it was more of a grey colour. On a dark day, when the
season was closing in, they were seen leaving the town like the
blue heron.

As children, we'd burrow into the hay
or move bales like building blocks, trapping
carpet snakes. Together saw Tad Hunter clutching
at the mangled stump of his arm, the auger crazy
with his blood. Once we nearly drowned in a silo of barley,
sinking further with every move, pulled out crying
by this old man who said we'd learnt our lesson & didn't need
punishing any further. Who said the same, when – riding
his motorbike – we hit the cattle grid & skewed
into the creek. And when we fed a pet sheep his premium seed
wheat & watched it die from pickle poisoning. Neighbours
called us feral kids – 'little bastards, getting their claws
into everythin', like locusts in the crop, nothin' can stop
'em.' It's true, we ran amok, but we did our chores
& didn't mean any harm – a chip
off the ol' block his dad would say to the town cop.
On a dark day, when the season was closing in,
they were seen leaving the town, married again.

In some ways it was like a world under glass – porous glass that let
in the creek and the birds and the weather and the children who'd
creep up to the house as a dare, the old people having *that* reputa-
tion for strangeness, but kept the pain in, petrified in the moment. The boy's death had cut it off from the outside world and it
existed in a twilight which not even the most determined seasons
cold breach. I never said much about him. I read a lot and kept to
myself. But even the brightest books seemed dull. The shadows of
the blue heron indelible on their pages. On a dark day, when the
season was closing in, they were seen leaving the town, like the
blue heron.

It was one of those days when the black
cockatoos were low-loping in a storm-stained sky
& the creek ran river-thick, scouring the red clay
banks & swamping the nests of water rats, & the track
up to the top gate was up to the axles with mud & a long trek
around the flooded paddocks was necessary, stray
sheep stuck firm, the silos damp & full of sprouted wheat,
that they both emerged in black raincoats & doggedly
made their way to town on foot. As word had spread, the main street
was lined with adults & children who thought they were in for a treat.
But the old couple didn't lift their heads, & neither led
the other as they marched like mourners or a parody of the dead,
marching a slow funereal slog towards the empty church.
A few moments later the priest appeared
& followed them into the silence beyond the arch.
On a dark day when the season was closing in,
they were seen leaving the town, married again.

Note: 'Blue heron' is a local nickname for the 'white-faced heron' – a bird that is
largely blue-grey.

RETURNING TO BICKLEY RESERVOIR PENDING ITS
REINTRODUCTION INTO PERTH'S MAINS WATER SUPPLY

Time's confidence ripples
out over the slaughter:
European carp & marron
writhe through the headlines,
reporters flicking stories
like corpses out of the virulent
slurry, as Bickley Reservoir
is drained & scoured.
A long-delayed autumn cracking
in plates along the unhealthy
banks, the crusty surface
crumbling like rust, seeping
into the carmine stream cutting
thinly its line to the drain-
hole:
            depth-of-field dictates
the construction crane has both
soft edges (&)
                        a prominence,
like the emblem
on a bonnet of an unfamiliar car,
or the gills of carp blown
to full-throttle position.
Cars cling to the fringes
of lookouts & carparks.
The old making way for the new,
they say. Corporeal the world
below the waterline, beyond
the stiff stand of bamboo:
                        car parts
& electrical equipment, smoking implements
& beer bottles, sandshoes & scarves,
deckchairs & rolls of telephone wire.
The sky is spilling over the hills

threatening to fill the tear-shaped
basin. The sky is colourless.
Kids throw stones at forty-fours
stranded near the wall: ricochet & soft
thud as projectiles are swallowed by mud.
A heavy-browed couple jigger
paralysed marron with a gidgee, shaking
them into a sodden sugarbag
that dragged between them ploughs
a vicious furrow.
            One of the kids
tells them the marron'll make 'em sick,
even the birds steer clear,
but they scream Piss Off! & persist.
The crane aches to move.
                  Water
cuts silently now – a few autumns
back it deadened calls between
bushwalkers, picnickers, & lovers,
& the reservoir's banks held tightly
the temporary & vanishing hours.

WATCHING THE STORM APPROACH
CANNING BRIDGE

Bottleneck or gateway? Where the Swan
& Canning rivers merge, or as the storm
approaches – a throng of poltergeists

with wicked notions – clash.
Hypnotised or possessed
they hesitate, & then suddenly

erupt as if struck by an irrepressible
freedom, a sundering of all morality.
Clouds hang over the city like strips

of greying flesh, the storm's breath
blown over the sulphurous, angry
waters. Beneath the bridge

irregular wooden pylons quiver,
& bait fish swim with a wind
that rushes against the tide

thundering through the channel, drawn by
the distant conjectural sea.
These silver minnows remain stationary

by swimming furiously, glittering brightly
just below the surface. Medusas –
camouflaged brown & khaki –

toss past like wind-struck parachutes.
A blowfish races through the school
of bait fish & eats voraciously. On the decking

deadly litters of blowfish corpses
begin their rapid rot-down.
The bait fish act as lures as the storm approaches,

their brilliance in the murky waters
enough to drag the inquisitive down. Their beauty
the beauty of the storm, now alive

with electricity – the blue light arcing out
over the city, sparking rods
on the city's tallest buildings.

Their beauty that of the transfigured –
stationary, yet vigorous in their stasis,
the undead – like a poem.

Another blowie bludgeons their ranks
& the wind drives the surface crazy.
It's as if they are atoms of one body:

these tiddlers explode as one, spray fuming
through the wind-slick, the body molten & singing
of Democritus. 'We are accustomed to speak

of heat, of cold, of colour. In reality
there are atoms & space.' Their
phonoaesthemic bodies obey the storm's

linguistic flare, flash, flicker, & flame.
There is a lull, as if the storm, transfixed over the city,
contemplates its course. I am possessed

by a torpor, I'm a child fishing here
with my brother, as guilty as the next kid –
stranding blowies in heaps on the deck.

We are watching older kids drink green
ginger wine & smoke Marlboroughs. Sometimes
fighting, marking their territory.

Old men drink from bottles
shrouded in brown paper bags & use
the smallest hooks & know all the tricks.

They seem never to move, but bury their catch
in dank hessian sacks. Sunlight breaks through temporarily
& as it nets you through the pylons you try to break free.

The storm stirs & a cormorant fillets
your body – a dark sonaric mass. The storm
tacks its way up the Swan, towards the Canning,

calling to all fish that move beneath
the bridge: O skippy, O tarwhine, O tailor & flounder,
O bream & KGs, O snook, O flathead & salmon,

O pike, O cobbler & you, great mulloway.
Those dead blowfish, looking like Jules Verne
submersibles – porthole eyes

& cyber bodies, living metal struck by a virus.
The bait fish ignite with the lightning,
the sky is as black as an epigraph.

LIGHTNING / TREMORS

META-LIGHTNING

from the *Concordance*

Exodus 19:16 'And it came to pass on the third day in the morning, that there were thunders and lightnings, and a thick cloud upon the mount, and the voice of the trumpet, exceedingly loud; so that all the people that *was* in the camp trembled.'

Matthew 24: 27 'For as the lightning cometh out of the east, and shineth even unto the west; so shall also the coming of the Son of man be.'

Luke 10: 18 'And he said unto them, I beheld Satan as lighting fall from heaven.'

John Berryman: 'And the lightning dances, but I cannot despair.'

1 SHEET — A MOCK EPIC

a conceit – the celestial attention seeker – the audacity
but not the ordinance to back it up – the long-lined

poem that gives a general impression
but doesn't strike a chord – a stock epithet

to tie the impression together – a conversation
in coffee shop or bar, politely passing the time

but using the jargon: chic, hip, 'in', witty.
like, he's threatening to come down

but just can't find the time.

2 HEAT

A festival of erotica. It's out there
on the horizon without any

of the threat – singing the evening
in its cornering the global curve,

a cruise ship with a ghost crew
entertaining the determined-to-enjoy-themselves

passengers, as we in deckchairs
talk of 'wild-fire' wondering

why such phenomena
refuse investigation.

3 FORK

The lens cannot capture the lightning
carving even the dark patches

between glowing city & Deep Water Point jetty.
This is the beginning & end of Heaven – that marooned

souls discharge from earth with a rush, like
a teleporter – though to keep the balance

Heaven dumps its waste. Trees explode,
wanderers are struck down, water electrified,

lightning conductors working hard as decoys.
As omen it pre-empts a death in the family, divorce,

scandal, difficult births, financial disaster, revolution,
war, the collapse of empires, & bad nerves.

But science & God infuse the struck body
leaving no room for despair.

BALL LIGHTNING AS MEDIUM

You can't evoke this one in a Leyden jar
unless a car in the nightblack atmosphere
works as an electrical condenser.

That you should chance upon this phenomenon
on an outback road after a sultry day's shearing,
eyes peeled for roos so easily hypnotised

by the eyebeams of cars – taking in light
& consequently de-illumined like inverted,
candescent globes. That this phenomenon

should make itself known on a bend of road
where a mate died a couple of months back,
that out there, deep in wheat & sheep country,

where stories of fireballs crashing into sun-
dried crops & dowsing them in sparks
that start no fires are accepted as fact,

death might hover as a brilliant blue-
white ball over the road, the living passing
between worlds in an instant, leaving

an after-image burning like *déjà vu*.

LIGHTNING TREE

It's stark white in this hard
winter light. At its base
brackish water spreads like exposed film
out through marshgrass & paperbarks –
a snapped bone, it punctures the skin.
On its splintered crown
the Great Egret stretches, its knifed beak
piercing the cold blue sky –
an inverted lightning strike
fielding its wings –
a crucifix – hesitating,
as if held by a magnet,
then dropping into flight,
dragging lightning rod legs.

IN EXPECTATION OF A LIGHTNING STRIKE
ON WIRELESS HILL

In expectation of a lightning strike
On Wireless Hill you sit and wait – a Passover
Sky brooding like tinfoil in smoke-bush –
Charged and ready to tap into the suburbs.
When asked where birds go during a storm
You can answer that it's here –
To this hill: cockatoos and rosellas
Clustering in the lower limbs of banksias
And eucalypts. You say to yourself
That this visit is purely scientific,
That it's *likely* a strike
Will happen here – the highest
Ground for miles around.
The road that rings the hill
Is like a black echo renewing
Its pulse towards extinction –
Like a rare species of flower rekindled
After having been 'lost forever'.
So you sit, earthed by observation and conjecture,
In expectation of a lightning strike
On Wireless Hill.

THE WILL-O'-THE-WISP

That in the night have lost their aim,
and after foolish fires do stray
'The Mower To The Glowworms'
                                    – Andrew Marvell

1 JACK O'LANTERN

Silly Jack O'Lantern
wandering on unwanted
low land like some
drunken bushman
with a hurricane lamp,
zigzagging against the indigo shades,
night-dank paperbarks –
their skins autumn-damp
& dead heavy, as mockingly
the tiny flame dances & disappears
only to reappear
nearby – the ague, bone-ache,
rheumatic territories
where its spryness mocks,
as the traveller follows
to its nameless crypt,
sinking-sand or swamp,
gully fetid with salt
& algae, the corpses
of foxes & the anatomies
of their prey, the atoms
of nomads & farmers
& the vapours
of their ancestors.

2 THE DRUNK TO THE WILL-O'-THE-WISP

You tiny flames, shining so bright
it's like you were sent to find me,
the dark so close & nightbirds quiet –
the ground rotten, air's perfidy.

Another whiskey & I'd be dead –
my lips pressed to the bottle's lips
I chanced on your crazy dance – you led –
a *pas de deux* deep into crypts

of trees, out past my ol' lady's grave,
past where my father & brother
lie, with a tracker's elusive
art. To some you might seem to wander,

though I know *you* know the way.
I know *you* know that amongst those trees
the voices of the lost waft silently
like whisky vapours, my prayers.

TREMORS: A REPORT

Some of us live willingly on faultlines.

'An earthquake which swept across the southern half of W. A. at 11 a.m.
yesterday flattened the wheatbelt town of Meckering (population 250), 84
miles north of Perth.'
                        West Australian, 15 October, 1968.

Eighty-four miles south of Meckering the metronome skipped a beat
                    & wandered across the piano,
paintings tilted & dried paint dripped to the floor. McCubbin's swagman
                lost a billy full of hot, strong tea.
We rushed from the house as the ground rippled like a mirage, or
heat waves on the road. My mother gripped my arm hard enough
                    to drive dark crescents deep
into flesh. Trees trembled while birds sat perfectly still,
as if balanced on gyroscopes. The dog cowered on the porch.

Pipes burst, houses collapsed, roads erupted, paddocks were
torn apart, railway tracks became fluid & whipped out like dugites
    sunning themselves on beds of warm blue metal, silos cracked –
    feed grain running like rivers through the openings – parrots,
strangely silent before the quake, clustered like emerald jewels
on the yellow halo about the ruins, gullies opened, chicken coops
were sprung, water tanks torn – their precious contents drained
    through shattered crusts of salt. Bridges blocked suddenly
                    empty creeks.

Townsfolk, it is said, hid under sinks & tables & stood in door-frames. The Civil Defence Service, CWA & Red Cross went straight into action. Tea & blankets & the chant *our town is no more let us rebuild our town is no more let us rebuild* which had the air of a mantra when droned in the wide-open spaces. And later their self-admonition *there had been tremors but we chose to ignore them there had been tremors but we chose to ignore them* which gradually became *there'd been tremors but we'd had them before there'd been tremors but who would have thought.* Though some wags from the Cunderdin Gliders' Club joked that it would have been safer riding thermals than turbulence on the stormy *terra firma.*

Wheatlands was only seven miles from the epicentre. The walls of the homestead fractured, paddocks opened, the surrounding hills convulsed. Auntie Elsie, custodian over the original Wheeler Homestead, watched as her house sank. Later she'd joke that its tilt was like the Leaning Tower of Pisa. My cousins slept in their car overnight. Afterwards, they found that dry wells had filled with water, freshwater wells had run dry or turned salt, soaks flooded into gullies, thickly-walled earthen dams had split & emptied out onto the paddocks carrying saplings like driftwood, that fences had been uprooted – wire snapping like overwound clock springs, that straw-thatched barns had become stooks in the houseyard. The horses were crazy for days & the chooks wouldn't lay. The York church held extra services & there were special collections for those hardest hit. At school the kids were full of it.

They've built a gazebo as memorial in Meckering. The Meckering
Agricultural Society (Inc) has brought out a souvenir booklet
full of maps, notes & photographs. They've rebuilt the town
three hundred metres south – imperial has long since
given way to metric – out of tin & steel-reinforced concrete. There
is a fledgling tourist industry. Everybody you talk to refers to the
silence of the birds on the morning before the quake.
They seem to need to talk with outsiders. Hadn't even seen a bird
that morning, a man balanced on a bicycle adds. His wife had called
it a storm beneath the ground. That it'd been like wading
through heavy surf. That people
had lost everything except ridiculous items like curtain fittings. That
they'd suffered complete derangement of the senses while the earth
was erupting. Date palms mark the site of the old town. There is
a memorial plaque & a pair of garden lions that feign vigilance.
Apparently there are up to five hundred tremors each year,
though only a few are felt – these rattle crockery & unsettle orn-
aments. Some of the older residents believe it is the unsteady
hand of the old lady who died of fear after the quake – assuring
herself that family dinner sets & nostalgic bric-a-brac are real,
not fragments mingled with dust in the ruins of her house.

CONFESSIONAL

BLUE BAGS / TALISMANS

Blue bags
strung from the arm
of the mangle
swing hypnotically
as the limp tongues
of shirts flop
from the machine's
red lips. My grandmother tells me
as she cranks and feeds
this creature with bad blood
that one day my auntie ended up
blue from head to foot.
She'd hidden behind the rockery
covered with mats of nasturtium flowers,
bees sparking in their cellophane hearts.
A man had chased her from school
and pursued her into the garden,
had searched long and hard
as she remained still and silent,
bees stings probing her skin
like sharpened raddlesticks.
Blue bags sucked the poison
from those wounds thirty
years back, and now
swing like talismans
of deliverance
amongst the loads
of laundry that fill
my grandmother's
memory.

DECEPTION & THE WEATHER STATION

High in the silky oak
where no adult could climb
& my brother on 'pain of death'
was forbidden to go – though in retrospect
probably did – I secured a bundle of instruments
(test tube with funnel as rain gauge,
coils of copper wire, a thermometer,
& a windvane that could only indicate
within a 270-degree range) in order
not to predict but accurately
determine the weather. There was no metaphor
to be made out of this. It was a straightforward case
of deception, unless deceiving is the shadow
all metaphors suggest. The child scientist
in me determines I must now report:
that to impress family & any
visiting friends, I'd chalk
on a board in the kitchen
the day's weather forecast.
No highs & lows, just
if it would rain & if so how much,
the temperature, the possibility
of wind & roughly at what speed.
Also the precise time
of sunrise & sunset, just to set the sceptics
right with some hard-edged research.
It worked. I gained much kudos
& was spoken about throughout
the neighbourhood. All radios & disused
telephones came my way, soon dismantled & turned into
a kind of house-to-house communication system.
And Christmas & birthdays would see electronic
& chemistry sets. But my future
was decided by deception – and here's the twist
made obvious in my writing this. Though

I've heard it said that all music & poetry
if good is based on sound mathematics.
My all-too-accurate predictions came care of a small
transistor radio – with earplug – kept under my bed.
I'd wake up before all else just to get the day's
weather. My exaggerated climb would
come after breakfast, the chalk board
already filling my head.

BRIDGING THE GAP: THE GAFF

When he went *north*
my father left
his reinforced
concrete shed, a steel box
packed with spanners
and jacks, the odd
engine block
unable to rot –
languishing
in bad blood;
star-eyed pigweed
and black, indelible sand;
a double-handed pitsaw
whose teeth had been wrenched
from the jaws
of a white pointer
in steel-blue waters
hypothermic off the southern coast;
his father's forestry
records – grid-locked and marked
in purple pencil; a couple of
bamboo fishing rods,
each three times
the length of his body
and slung between Meccano-like
roof supports
eyes hanging
loosely;
a wicked gaff,
simple but effective –
a section of bamboo
a shark hook
rings of bronze
swathes of insulation tape

bridging the gap
between beach
and sea;
an insurance policy;
a marriage licence –
the savagery of vows
made as the bait
was taken calmly.

THE WEATHER BOX

It was she of the storms,
he of the glorious day.
On the he days she – my step-
grandmother that is – would sit
on the toilet, door wide open,
facing the sun, legs spread
so the grey coil of her
shadowy interior leapt out
at us brazenly. She would call
us brothers to her throne
and say, 'Today is the little
man's day, she remains indoors
sulking after the dampness
of late Autumn, or conjuring
tempests out of heat drawn
suddenly over the sea,
her fury multiplying
when a dry thunder
teases in the distance
and the little man continues
to smile, wielding his scythe
and airing his summer breeches.'
One day she of the storms
poked her nose out of her
shuttered Swiss cottage, cloak
nipped close to her breast,
pale cheeks shimmering
like ghosts, and our
step-grandmother
declared it was time
to steal away her two
darling grandsons.
Parked out the front
of our school she coaxed

through the rain. We lifted
our bright yellow coats close
to our ears and ran – two
small suns flickering
in the eyes of the storm.

APPROACHING THE ANNIVERSARY OF MY LAST
MEETING WITH MY SON

I never write 'confessional' poetry
but your voice – like forked lightning
etching a thunder-dark river – leaves me
no choice but to speak directly.
I hear your mother laugh.
That I've screened myself
in the ash of burnt images,
left nothing intact behind.
It's almost the anniversary
of my leaving, and you don't
know my voice on the phone
when you ring Nanna.
Told it's Daddy,
you say, 'I'd better go,'
your mother erupting
from another room;
it's not safe using the phone
during a storm. And peace
is as important at home
as food and warmth, so I let it go.
Sometimes I sit on Deep Water Point jetty
and remember the time we spent
considering what lies below
the glistening surface,
what drives mottled brown jellyfish
in scattered flotillas
to beach themselves,
why herons strut their stuff
curious yet suspicious –
having to answer to no more
than the weather,
small fish, and an urge to be free.

DEED OF TITLE: THE LOWER REACHES OF
THE CANNING RIVER

Being by a river is being in many places at once.

As a child I *owned* the stretch between Bull Creek
and Canning Bridge. I still like to think it's *mine*.
I feel uneasy when people say they are going to *write
the river*. What would they know? Did they
get angry when the man at Spinaway Crescent
drove a star picket into the heart of a dermatitic
paperbark so he could tether a dinghy? Or throw a line
into its cool waters every evening, even when storm-light
cracked across the city, charged the current deeply?
Did they row to the far bank? Or risk ear, nose and throat
infections by swimming when summer made it sick
with algae? Or keep notes on waterbirds, look for the sign
of a rare species? Did they write in their first diary – 'despite
being confined to my room I climbed out into the day
and ran all the way to the river'? – a lock-and-key pocket-
book with a cloth cover and an antiquarian map of the world.
A diary which became a journal because the words broke free
of the days. Where words flowed free in a good season
and fell stagnant when heat sucked its life dead dry.
Where stability measured itself as a sand anchor set
against a slowly retreating tide at sunset, kingfish cold
and sleek against the dry-ice fizz of froth cut in its race for the sea.
Is it to them a place where they chanced on a kiss? An opportune
place for a moment's respite from the domestic lie?
The office? The traffic thicker than any malignant aquatic
growth? Well then, let them *think* they own it. Sold
to the highest bidder – like houses that have crept quietly
down the banks until they have eroded its flow a little more.
The post-meridian moon is too bright – the river is at its core!

Serpentine. Tracy asks me to stop
at the cemetery – her brother
who drowned in Wungong Dam
is buried here. She clears
dry leaves from the framed
blue metal while I think
of Craig whose grave
I've never visited.
It's just something I can't face.
Though I'll wander almost happily
amongst the tombs of those I've
not known. I did not know
Tracy's brother, and it shows.
I set out in search of flowers.
It is autumn and they are scarce.
Behind the cemetery I come across
lines of dead sheep. Wool, red
with raddle paint, hangs
dankly about the carcasses.
I return empty handed.
One can't transfer flowers
from another's grave.
At the right time of year
Tracy says kangaroo paws
are rampant – occasionally
erputing from graves,
bloody windchimes
muttering under their breaths.

TENEBRAE

for Tracy

You are on the verge
of a resurrection,
standing on a fragile shoreline,
erosion undermining
the limestone cliff face,
expecting to plunge suddenly
into the churning ocean.
You'd rebuild memories,
though this coastline
is always changing – a childhood
hiding place eroded,
an overhang collapsed
like the tide. Those
limestone columns
reaching towards a god
that would take your past
as if it were an offering.
But though the lights
one by one extinguish
as you explore deeper,
that final light – the sun –
grows stronger,
despite the coming winter,
the darkening seas.

SUBLIMINAL MESSAGES

INNER TRUTHS

The air thicker than the Thames.
It is not a good day for cherries

which ripen too fast, uncomfortably.
They draw you in. Red dwarfs

collapsing into black holes
as you, outflung on the spindly

arms of the nebulae, can't get
to them in time. But then

you know that nothing much can
really hurt them and that their

strength will multiply through experience.
The inner truth inundates & the room

fills with their mist. Here, new atoms
are created & they run off you

like streams of perspiration.

INDELIBLE

The light drones
like the car radio –
metallic & maroon,
while rust rivets
thickets of dock
deep in the shallow pan
of paperbarks – an island
below the worn parapets
of hills smoking lead
& cobalt.
                    In a subdued
& hazy voice
signalman Hardingham
talks of locals in a Cambodian
village shooting indelible
clouds to quench a fire,
or maybe I've put voice
to the neutral ink
of the morning paper.
                    An
ibis moves through earth-smoke
as a chipped moon emits
its lousy late-afternoon ambience,
the sun stagnant & stranded
among the paperbarks. I wonder
if its flight has cut
my path before.
                    It passes
& the sun drops
suddenly.
                    Loss shadows the road
& the car drives itself.

THE GENETICS OF FILM

A blue cow wanders fields
of grass spliced with plastic
(set nicely, the plastic
is blooming), in the distance
featherless wingless chickens
hum the artificial weather, the current
of uncertain evenings. The clouds,
tinged crimson, roll & flicker
about the batteries & research stations
like brittle film, frame by frame
the sepia scratched & fading,
though archivists work
day & night with new techniques
designed to prolong existence:
new depth & even unheard-
of-colours. In these old films
there are Jersey cows
& feathered chickens.

SOLITARY ACTIVITIES

He spent his working hours deflating words
and every Saturday he spied on birds.
        'Mars Sonnet No. 5' – Peter Porter

Poetry is not the only thing
That you can 'do' alone in a room;
You could, like Andrew Crosse,
Imagine living creatures
Created by electrical currents
                        passing
Through brilliant chemical mixtures
The colour of tropical birds.
                Or believe
That Morely Martin, alone in *his* room,
Produced 'primordial protoplasm'
From fossil-free Azoic Rock;
                        but that's what
Comes with reading dictionaries
Of Common Fallacies and being alone
Yourself – the weekday air thick with words,
The weekend call of birds a long way off.

SUBLIMINAL MESSAGES

The residue of flowerings – oleanders
crimson pink cerise on freeway islands
softening the harsh suncrack of metal
and glass, traffic caught in the melting.

Grasshoppers disperse with every step,
wasps frenzy about their chambers,
poems take the fifth column and file
notes in birth registries, obituaries.

River, mirror-poised, could be a dead
thing also – the shadows of pylons
as stable as slivers of ice; water,
molten extract of the suburbs, mere seepage.

Where datura bells hang limp-headed,
tolling in the dank airs, and morning glory
in topiaried rills creeps slowly beneath jets
with their oozing spinnerets crisscrossing

grey sky, the litter mulches of zamia palms,
stand on stand of bamboo, horses agisting
to the traffic, New York graffiti, and earth
movers levelling sights on hills, stands

of she-oak and eucalypt, the gun-grey quarry
bleeding the blue blood of the scarp dry.
Where subliminal messages are carried
by kerosene tractors ripping the summer's

firebreaks, children plundering orange trees,
the sinking asphalt. And where all the while
lives are drawn in the song of their bones –
bleached brittle, breaking the flesh, stretched.

THE RIBBON GUM

Stripped down to its bare trunk
like a paper lantern hanging
out of season, the bark of ribbon gum
is dark in the morning of a black sun.
A resident of this place lures
the bower birds with varying
intensities of blue, but the mountain
sky won't buy it, remaining dark
and indifferent to the call of intruders
as if everything blue is being sucked
into the exposed flesh of the ribbon gum,
the truth of its dark colourings
lying in lashes of screed
over the dull tesserae
of the garden.

OBELISKS

for Rod Mengham

Hay bales like stele or crypts
or the residue of sun
in a sea of Horus's wheat
like stone ships friezing
sun-driven hydraulics,
the Avon River running
darkly through the valley.
Totemic and primal they
lean into their shadows,
the blonde floor of harvest
anti-descriptive in emblematic
overtone, heat listless
at their bases: these uprights
of antipodean stonehenges
temporal and mocking
the chthonic source of their
construction, commodities
that might explode with heat.
Cyclical and ephemeral
the hawk that dives for skinks
in their vicinity, always cockatoos
perched like gargoyles –
eyes twisted to leers in masks
that require a duration
of references to be made
acceptable. The pattern
of the machine as it configures
the paddock, space contradicting
the brief time they persist sub-
consciously, rolling there
like chaotic empires

nearing the end of their days,
their situations as delicate
as the southern forest's
burnt orange haze, burnback
darkening catastrophe's fuel
like a dare, while nearby
stookers build ricks –
small offerings in fields
of obelisks gloating under
skies known for lightning,
the arsonist's glint.

DISSERTATION ON A WASP'S NEST

Who that has Reason, and his Smell
Wou'd not among Roses and Jasmin dwell?

              – Cowley

1

Striking deep into the crisp
salvers of dead jasmine flowers
the paper wasp outpaces
the eye –
the elapsed witherings
of its avionics,
high-pitched and devastating.

2

The rest of a paper wasp – thin grey
parchment chambers
moving towards opacity
bloom from a common
point, anchored stiffly
against the scent
of jasmine.

3

The wasp is the part
of a nest that flies.
Its wings the harp
on which frenzied
lullabies are cut.

4

A tiger with yellow stripes
would prefer to remain still
amongst the foliage,
watch as you pass confidently
by.
       As evening settles
like a fusty blanket, summer
heat pricking even the space
between carapace and flesh,
the wasps move slowly
over the nest's chambers.
Even the full moon
lifting its yellow eye
over the rim of the fence
cannot revitalise them.
The pull of the sun
cannot be mimicked.

5

To separate a wasp's nest
from the jasmine – fierce
undertaking I should refuse,
but wishing to preserve
both it and my child's
inquisitive
and vulnerable flesh,
I seek merely
to transfer
to a place
safer for both.
Two wasps
and a nest

in a coffee jar,
an impression
in the moon's
limp light.

6

Moisture
from night waterings
lifts the lawns
and gardens
in the early morning.
Wasps' fire
in the coffee jar,
their nest precarious
on its glass floor,
holdfast swimming
the petrified current.

A SECOND DISSERTATION ON A
WASP'S NEST

1 NOMENCLATURE

It is the time for planting
balsam & celosia, marigold & petunia,
sweet william & verbena,
lantana & juniperus,
myoporum & grevillea,
tomato & jasminum
polyanthum.

It is time to dig
the memory's fertile beds,
catch the raucous
peals of black cockatoos
& hope for a break
in the weather,
to observe the single cell
of a paper wasp queen expand
into a bell, its cells
holding the first group
of workers.

2 PREDESTINATION

That each year the new queen
builds under the eaves,
the germ of her empire
invisible through winter –
that even catastrophe
(such as gardener or house painter
removing her nest) will not prevent
the same spot being used by
another – each colony

sharing silent links,
enjoying a collective security –
that they were & are
meant to be there.

3 THE PERFUMED GARDEN – I.M.M (A LOST LOVE)

There is no jasmine in this garden
to remind me of you, & despite its lushness
no scent that stirs old memories. Wasps
communicate by odours you know – pheromones –
a word that sounds guardedly sexual.
The body fluids of some people
attract them, others send them crazy –
deodorants, soaps & certain sweet foods
send attractive messages
that ultimately lead to a frenzy
of sensual frustration.
I cannot segregate wasps
from thoughts of you,
regardless of the surroundings.
And the symbol of our love
was always poison,
the sting. You the wasp
that can strike repeatedly & survive,
I the bee whose one sting
is fatal only to the hypersensitive
& itself.

Lightning gravitates
between ground
& thunderhead:
the dark bodies
of wasps almost
neon – charged
by thunderbolts.
The paper bell tolls
& wings flick
like static & then as the dark
silence between flashes
smothers the nest
they slip back into stasis.
Again & again –
like a faulty power point –
they throw out
the occasional blue spark
& then, as the storm passes
& humidity gives way
to a cool change
they lose
their spark.
Winter approaches.
The nest diminishes
& I forget to make
my daily observations.

5 EVOLUTION & EXTINCTION

It's not the time for planting
a winter garden
though it's near.

Seeds in their cells
are germinating
& soon will be allotted
their place in the rich beds.
To plant out now
would be premature.

I busy myself with annuals:
calendula (for healing),
delphinium & ageratum,
viola & cineraria,
the reliable *forget-me-not*.

The wasps are slow now,
the last batch of workers
crawls slowly over
the uncapped cells.
I record my observations.
Soon I shall retire
& analyse this data
from a season of evolution
& extinction.

JOHN KINSELLA was born in Perth in 1963. He studied at the university of Western Australia and travelled extensively through Europe, the Middle East and Asia. He is a prolific writer and author of over 25 books, and has published poems in literary journals internationally and has received a number of literary awards, including a Young Australian Creative Fellowship and a two-year Fellowship from the Literature Fund of the Australia Council.

In 1998, he took up residence in the UK, where he is Fellow of Churchill College, Cambridge University. He is also Adjunct Professor to Edith Cowan University, Western Australia and Professor of English at Kenyon College in the United States.

Since 1998, he has been International Editor for Arc Publications, with whom he has published two previous collections, the first of which – *The Undertow: New and Selected Poems* (Arc, 1996) – was his first UK edition. His second collection for Arc, *The Silo: A Pastoral Symphony* (1997) was followed in 1999 by *Landbridge: An Anthology of Contemporary Australian Poetry* (also published by Arc in conjunction with Fremantle Arts Centre Press), which he edited.